GREAT RAILWAY PHOTOGRAPHERs

MAURICE EARLEY

Presented by Colin Garratt

from the collections of the National Railway Museum

Copyright ©1996 text and design Milepost 92¹/₂

This edition first published in 1996 by Milepost Publishing in association with Arcturus Publishing Limited

for

Selectabook
Folly Road, Roundway, Devizes, Wilts. SN10 2HR

Milepost Publishing is a division of Milepost 92¹/₂
Colin Garratt's audio-visual/video production,
photographic service and picture library for the railway industry.
Milepost also conserves and markets historic collections of negatives and transparencies

Designed by Milepost and Just My Type.

Printed and bound in Great Britain

ISBN 1 900193 60 4

Milepost 92¹/₂
Newton Harcourt
Leicestershire
LE8 9FH
Tel 0116 2592068

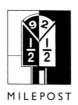

MILEPOST

PREVIOUS PAGE : *A West of England express from Waterloo in the four track section between Pirbright Junction and Basingstoke in early B.R. days. The locomotive is an unrebuilt Merchant Navy Class 4-6-2 No. 35009 'Shaw Savill' in the first B.R. standard blue livery. The signals were semi-automatic pneumatic installed c.1905. (226/96)*

INTRODUCTION
by Colin Garratt

Maurice W. Earley is one of the best loved railway photographers; his endearing and highly concentrated pictures have provided inspiration for over half a century. He took his first photograph in 1913 and began railway photography on 27th March 1922. His first picture was published in the Railway Magazine in 1925 showing the G.W.R. Royal Train near Maidenhead. Thenceforth M.E. was destined to publish prolifically.

He has always been associated with the Great Western and especially with Sonning Cutting and the Reading area. He took pictures in these places for over half a century and it was this familiarity, combined with his relentless pursuit for perfection, which enabled him to create masterpieces which have never been bettered. He would spend a whole day at one location perhaps for only one picture.

ABOVE: Sonning Cutting just east of Reading on the Great Western Railway's main line from Paddington was with-out doubt Maurice Earley's favourite location for photography. To start us off there we have a down express for Bristol and Taunton hauled by 'Castle' Class 4-6-0 No. 504x, the last figure is not visible on the print. It must have been a very hot day as the distant signal is not in the full off position due to the expansion of the wire. (B3050)

M.E.planned his photography meticulously; the direction of wind; the line and the location of intrusions such as lineside poles. He preferred to work in spring and autumn. His ideal weather was when the sky had white fluffy clouds, especially after rain, when these clouds reflect a great deal of light into the shadow portions of the train.

As M.E. stated: "A west to east line presents far more problems with regard to lighting than one which runs north to south. In the former case the sun is in the ideal position - 45 degrees to the train and behind the photographer - for short periods only during the day. Both the G.W.R. from Paddington to beyond Reading and the Southern from Waterloo to Basingstoke and Salisbury are in the east / west category; the principal up expresses have the sun on their tails in the afternoon and the down trains catch the sun head on".

The nuances of light direction and wind are summed up in M.E.'s account of the picture of "The Bristolian" seen on Goring troughs seen on the rear jacket. M.E. writes: "When I left home that evening it was dull and raining but I took the camera with me just in case. As I got down to the troughs, the sun came out in a rift between the clouds and shone brilliantly for about ten minutes, just long enough to get this shot, and then it vanished for the rest of the day; the dark clouds and the spray of water from the scoop made the picture".

M.E. was greatly inspired by F.E. Mackay, with whom he made many trips to locations at Kenton and Hadley Wood over the years from 1924/7. It was Mackay's influence that led M.E. to prefer press cameras and glass plate negatives. He ranged from the use of $3^1/2$ x $2^1/2$ to 5 x 4 - the quality of these was breathtakingly good quickly earning him the reputation of being a superb technician.

In 1922 M.E. founded the Railway Photographic Society. This was a circulating portfolio group in which members assessed and commented upon each others work. He ran R.P.S. for over 50 years and the organisation did much to advance the art of railway photography.

His first love was photographing trains at speed, although he did modify this approach to please model makers for detailed photographs of prototypes and older designs - the types usually found in sheds and yards rather than out on the main lines. He also included fascinating aspects of railway operations; the slip coach sequence included in this volume being an example.

As far as his trains were concerned, he was most attracted by expresses; freights featured far less as did secondary lines. The old and threatened were not as fashionable for documentation then as they are today in our age of rapid change. He loved clean, flamboyant trains snaking their way across the landscape. The train was sharp from engine to last coach thanks to a swing back facility on his camera.

Writing in 1950 Maurice Earley commented on two significant factors relating to his photography. First the advance in the speed of plates and films and secondly the improvements in their tonal qualities. He also mentions the inordinate amount of time and effort railway photography takes, ranging from planning locations, physically getting to them with heavy cameras and glass plates, shooting the right picture in all the nuances and uncertainties associated with railway photography through to processing his films and, of course, printing them, which involved tremendous dedication and concentration when aiming for perfection.

He paid ready tribute to photographers during the early years of the present century saying that, "present day photographers (1950s) can scarcely appreciate the handicaps which their counterparts of past years had. Fine grain developers were at an experimental stage; speed of plates and films was not even one fifth of present values whilst the contrast of those early films and plates would strike terror into the hearts of anyone working today. All highlights such as skies, boiler tops and smoke effects with white steam were prone to be lost completely". Indeed during his early years M.E. often

4

spent a whole evening trying to get a reasonable print from one contrasty negative. He summed up by saying "It is just as easy to produce an ideal negative in 1951 as it was difficult in 1925".

Between 1935 and 1939 M.E., along with his wife and a full quota of plates and Ordnance Survey maps, undertook a series of memorable photographic tours by car covering much of Britain. It was not unusual to cover up to 2,000 miles in a fortnight.

His memoirs of these expeditions make poignant reading; travelling as far north as Dingwall he found a Jones Goods reposing in the depot yard amid the pouring rain; his first visit to Shap and how he nearly forgot to work the shutter at the sight and sound of a Princess Royal Pacific toiling up the famous grade with the Royal Scot; Gresley's Mikado "Cock of the North" at Aberdeen; visiting Gresham box on Beatock and discovering the spot which Hamilton Ellis had used as the location for his famous picture of Cardean on the Corridor; the desolation of the Pennines at Ais Gill, with Wild Boar Fell looming behind the up trains - "so profound was the silence that the bleating of sheep often made one jump and people's voices which seemed only yards away actually came from farms a mile distant".

ABOVE : *West of the A4 road bridge (also seen from the other side on page 3) a 'Hall' Class 4-6-0 No. 4917 'Crosswood Hall' is on an express on the down relief line. The main train seems to consist of nine or ten coaches all with roof destination boards plus two corridor thirds added on the front for additional accommodation. This is described as a West Midland train so may well have had portions for Hereford and Wolverhampton splitting off at Worcester Shrub Hill. (826)*

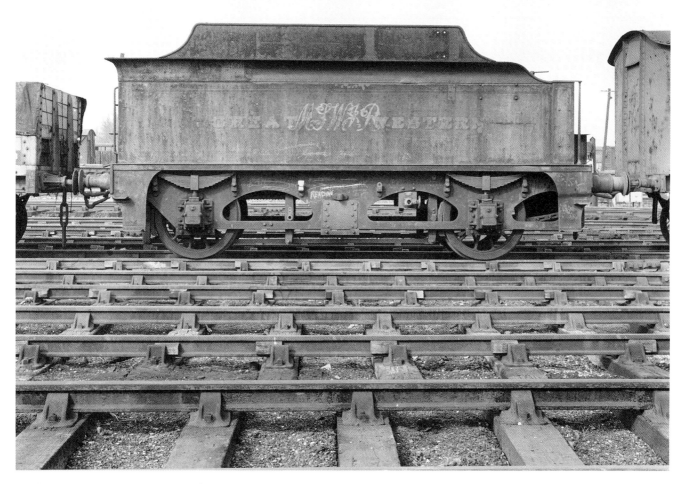

ABOVE : *All railways were thrifty and reused redundant items whenever possible. When the Midland and South Western Junction Railway's 4-4-0s were withdrawn in the 1930s five of their tenders were converted to mobile water tanks. The centre pair of wheels was removed, buffers and draw gear fitted at the locomotive end and a discharge pipe and tap fitted which is visible behind the leading wheels. The G.W.R. paint has weathered and the M. & S.W.J.R. monogram is clearly visible. (F4/74)*

Derbyshire's tunnels and viaducts also fascinated him; the first railway picture he ever saw was of a train in the Chevin Valley and he found exactly the same spot and made a famous picture of a Compound in a scene which had changed little. He recalled Morthoe Bank on the Ilfracombe line, where he lost one of his best shots through a grass snake crawling across his feet; he joined the long tradition of railway photographers who have visited the sea wall at Teignmouth, whilst August Saturdays on the Somerset and Dorset Joint, with its curves, gradients and double headed trains was a perennial joy.

On his forays far and wide the loading and packing up of used plates was done in many diverse places; under the bedclothes, in wardrobes and cupboards, after the hotel lights were out or in so called dark rooms in Chemists.

He loved the streamlined era of the 1930s; the spotless trains with their wonderful colour schemes. Their speed enthralled him too; camera shutters now had to be accurate and he remembers being "keyed up" to press the shutter at the precise instant to catch a train moving at hitherto unknown speeds.

The advent of World War Two meant the curtailment of railway photography but in 1943 M.E. was given permission to take pictures under certain restrictions. This resulted in his famous pictures of American S160s - which he rightly predicted at the time "will become very valuable negatives".

After the war, M.E became very active photographically to catch up on six lost years. He was friendly with O.S. Nock who resumed his footplate journeys after the war and whenever he was travelling in the Reading area he would ask M.E. to photograph the train. O.S. Nock's footplate journeys were both legendary and prolific and M.E. took up the challenge with vigour, frequently going to business complete with camera and equipment in order to get the relevant pictures. Invariably he would have to take some time off work, returning an hour or two later as though nothing had happened! He found these diversions pleasant and stimulating. The locomotive exchanges of 1948 were another source of much inspiration.

Between 1925 and 1950 M.E. estimated that he took ten thousand pictures. A vast number were duplicates taken in his attempt to perfect particular scenes of locations or locomotive types. A lot of these "inferior negatives" were scrapped in his quest for perfection but 3,265 are currently held by the N.R.M. whose former Technical Information Officer, John Edgington, has provided the captions for this book. John, who began as a professional railway man with the L.M.S. in1942, has an all round knowledge of railways matched by few individuals living today and I am much indebted to him.

ABOVE : *Maurice Earley obviously had good connections with Paddington and he was granted a photographic permit during the darkest days of the 1939-45 war. This was very fortuitous as he managed to record some of the unusual workings around Reading. Possibly the most interesting strangers were the United States Army Transportation Corps 2-8-0s many of which worked in England and Wales prior to 'D-Day'. USA2131 is seen at Reading in 1943 as a class 'H' freight or mineral train. (M/5013)*

In the days before mass road transport for nearly everything, racehorses were conveyed by rail to and from meetir number of important race courses some with their own stations open only on race days (e.g. Cheltenham and Newk the train plus four passenger coaches. The reason for the latter is not obvious as, except for one vehicle for the guard, one of the last Great Western 2-4-0s in service and the last class to have 'sandwich' frames, two steel plates encasing

...d many owners and/or trainers had dedicated horse boxes inscribed with their names. The Great Western served a ...horse box special is pictured here on 1 August 1926 probably running to Newbury. There are fourteen horse-boxes in ...ooms travelled in a half compartment in the horse box which is visible in the first box. The locomotive is of interest being ...od filling.(C04/177)

With few exceptions, M.E.'s photography had to be done during holidays and weekends; he travelled little on business. He never attempted to photograph each locomotive in the country (as did H.C.Casserley) because he was interested in the whole train and one engine of a class usually looked much like another. M.E. combined a keen interest in railways with a keen interest in photography and was ever keen to help up and coming photographers.

My personal assessment of him would be to say that no other photographer conveys so well the atmosphere of the moment in which the picture was taken; one almost senses the temperature whilst the smell of the earth and of the railway itself seeps out of his pictures.

In his final years M.E. was primarily confined to home having virtually lost the use of his legs, but his spirit and enthusiasm for railways and photography never dimmed. He died on 15th November 1982 at his home in Reading.

Many thanks to the National Railway Museum for providing access to the largest photographic archive in Britain. Milepost also wish to thank the staff at the N.R.M. who are involved in this series.

Colin Garratt,
Milepost 92½,
Newton Harcourt,
Leicestershire,
September 1996

RIGHT, above : *The Great Western Dynamometer car was used for testing locomotives in road conditions and, in addition to Great Western engines, in B.R. days, some from other regions were tested. In February and March 1953 ex-London and North Eastern Railway Class V2 2-6-2 No. 60845 ran trials on the G.W.R. The trail train is seen here at Scours Lane Junction west of Reading on 4 March. It had left Reading for Stoke Gifford near Bristol at 10.52 hauling 25 coaches weighing 762 tons. The train is crossing from relief to main lines at Scours Lane. (15/53)*

RIGHT, below: *Scours Lane again on 4 March 1953 with the 11.15 am Paddington to Bristol on the main line hauled by 'Castle' class 4-6-0 No. 5082 'Swordfish'. This locomotive was originally named 'Paris Castle' and was one of twelve which were renamed in 1940/1 after combat aircraft of World War 2. (13/53)*

ABOVE : *The Great Western Railway was a pioneer in the use of diesel railcars having a maximum of 38 bogie vehicles. The first 16 were used on semi-fast and express services including three with buffets for a Birmingham-Cardiff service via Stratford on Avon and Gloucester. No 17 was a parcel car for use in the London area including J. Lyons' traffic from Park Royal. These cars were single units without buffers and or draw gear (except for use in an emergency). Nos 18-34 had standard buffers and screw couplings and could haul a trailer. They were generally used on branch lines. No 34 was also a parcel car. Nos 35/6 and 37/8 were single ended cars and ran as a three car train with and intermediate trailers gangwayed throughout. Here one of the branch line cars leaves Great Shefford on the Lambourn Valley branch from Newbury. (157/52)*

ABOVE : *A close up of No. 1 engine on railcar No. 33 at Reading in 1952. (19/52)*

BELOW : *The Reading Society of Model Engineers hired one of the earlier Diesel railcars, No. 15, for a trip on the Lambourn Valley branch in 1952. It is seen here at Welford Park with the members enjoying themselves by displaying impossible signal indications no doubt by trying their strength on the balance weights on the signal post. (129/52)*

ABOVE : *Now for a brief look at the other three of the big four. The London and North Eastern contribution is the up 'Flying Scotsman' leaving Potters Bar tunnel in 1937. The locomotive is class A4 No. 4492 'Dominion of New Zealand', one of five of the class selected for working 'The Coronation' between Kings Cross and Edinburgh and named after the five largest countries of the British Empire. Those not working 'The Coronation' were used on other important expresses such as the non-stop 'Flying Scotsman'. The G.N. somersault signal is shortly to be replaced by a three aspect colour light. (G3502)*

Four Views at Reading West Junction

PREVIOUS PAGES left, above : *Another wartime photograph and another stranger on Great Western metals. For use exclusively in Britain all four of the main line railways built 2-8-0s to the L.M.S. class 8F design. The G.W.'s contribution was 80 built at Swindon, L.M.S. Nos 8400 to 8479. No 8428 is on the down relief line with a 'through freight' composed of bogie wagons loaded with tree trunks in 1944. (M5031)*

PREVIOUS PAGES left, below : *USA 2-8-0 No. 2339 is coming off the curve from the Berks and Hants line and crossing to the down relief line. This again is a 'through freight' with a variety of open wagons and covered vans. The year is 1943. ((M5004)*

PREVIOUS PAGES right, above : *An ordinary passenger train on the down relief line hauled by a Churchward two cylinder Saint class 4-6-0 No. 2902 'Lady of the Lake'. This was the first modern express class on the G.W.R. from which the four cylinder class developed. The train is the 11 am Sundays from Paddington and the year 1928. ((H3612)*

PREVIOUS PAGES left,below :

Another 'Saint' class 4-6-0 No. 2908 'Lady of Quality' on the down main line with a train of empty milk tanks for West Wales in 1943. Most of London's milk was carried by rail from concentration points in Wales and the West Country direct to depots owned by the big dairies (United, Express etc). Each dairy owned its own tanks while the railways owned the chassis.(M5006)

Two Southern Views

ABOVE : *The down Atlantic Coast Express at Battledown Flyover en route to Devon and Cornwall in 1949. The locomotive, No. 35005 'Canadian Pacific', appears to be in a hybrid livery probably malachite green with British Railways in full and the number in Southern Railway style. The coaches are Bulleid post-war corridor and saloon stock which were comfortable but seated four aside in the third class compartments. (74/49)*

BELOW :
An up West of England express again at Battledown Flyover in 1946. The up Bournemouth line crosses on the steel girder bridge immediately above the two leading coaches. This is a Saturday train as it carries a reporting number, 321, hung from the top lamp bracket of Lord Nelson class 4-6-0 No. 859 Lord Hood. (5143)

ABOVE : In steam days Locomotive depots were extremely dangerous and dirty places in which to work with coal dust and ash flying about and oil and water under foot. Camden shed, the principal London Midland Region passenger depot in London, which supplied power for the expresses from Euston is typical. The man on the frame of an unidentified Jubilee Class 4-6-0 is shovelling char from the smoke box into trolleys in the pit between the rails where it is being sprayed with water to keep down the dust. The trolley will later be hoisted up into the concrete tower above the locomotive and the contents tipped into a wagon for disposal elsewhere. There are numerous fire irons lying about which are also a potential hazard. The signal box in the background is Camden No. 1. An interior shot appears on page 37.

RIGHT : *The gloom and murk of a typical steam locomotive depot is portrayed in this shot of the front end of G.W. 4 cylinder 'Star' class 4-6-0 No. 4041 Prince of Wales photographed in the Bristol Bath Road shed in 1949. The building shows signs of neglect as did so much of the railway infrastructure in the post-war years. (M3/49)*

RIGHT : *A close up of the leading axle box with cover removed on the bogie of a Great Western 'King' class 4-6-0. The number stamped on the end of the axle indicates that the locomotive was No. 6007 but this may have been exchanged during overhaul. '70 Tons' may be the limit to which the axle was tested when new. (229/96)*

Four Views of Maurice Earley's favourite location, Sonning Cutting. It has been reported that the Great Western Railway built a fenced-in platform from which he could photograph in safety on the south side of the line between the single arch and the A4 bridges. It certainly appears that two of these pictures could have been taken from such a location.

ABOVE : *An up Ocean Liner Express from Plymouth Millbay to Paddington with 'Castle' Class 4-6-0 No. 4094 'Dynevor Castle' in charge. The three leading vehicles are 70 ft 'Ocean Mails' storage vans although they appear to have been demoted as there is no legend on the lower panels and they are probably conveying passengers' luggage. The nearer bridge, which is prominent in many of his photographs, carries a minor road from Woodley to the A4 and the A4 bridge is the one in the middle distance. (894)*

RIGHT: *A very lucky shot west of the A4 road bridge. A 'King' class 4-6-0 hauling a Taunton-Paddington express on the up main overtakes an ordinary passenger train on the up relief line with 'Castle' Class 4-6-0 No. 4083 'Abbotsbury Castle'. The leading vehicle of the express is also a 70ft 'Ocean Mail' van with a guard's compartment. (DH117)*

ABOVE : *Two down expresses between the minor road and the A4. The first is the Torbay Express of 13 or 14 coaches behind 'King' class 4-6-0 No. 6020, King Henry IV. (H3615)*

BELOW : *The train in the lower picture is a much shorter formation, six coaches only, and is the second portion of the Cornish Riviera Express. In 1938 streamlining was all the rage and the Great Western Railway, not wishing to be left out, modified a King and a Castle by fitting bulbous smoke box doors and sheet metal skirting over the front end and cylinders. This was completely useless and was soon removed, albeit piecemeal, restoring the two locomotives to their former elegance. No 5005 'Manorbier Castle' is seen retaining its bulbous nose and straight splasher and name plate but with most of the other skirting removed. (H3613)*

Maurice Earley ventured off the Great Western and Southern Railways during his annual holidays and here we have three pictures on the London Midland and Scottish Railway.

BELOW : *A famous and nowadays a much photographed location. This was taken in 1939 when Maurice Earley no doubt had the full length of the Settle and Carlisle line to himself. Approaching Ais Gill summit from Carlisle is the 12.10 pm Glasgow St Enoch to St Pancras with L.N.E.R. coaches from Edinburgh Waverly and immediately behind the train engine two loaded milk tanks from Appleby to Cricklewood. The load must be substantial as the train is double headed. The assistant engine is the first L.M.S. built three cylinder compound No. 1045 and the train engine a Class 5XP 'Jubilee' 4-6-0 No. 5562 'Alberta'. (L3719)*

RIGHT, above : *In July 1937 the L.M.S. introduced a high speed train from Euston to Glasgow and vice versa in 6½ hours named 'The Coronation Scot' in honour of the coronation of King George VI. The up train was photographed on Dillicar troughs (Westmorland) in 1937 hauled by 4 cylinder 4-6-0 No. 6222 'Queen Mary'. The livery was blue with silver bands along the coach and locomotive sides coming to a 'V' on the front of the streamlined casing. (L3703)*

RIGHT, below : *Into Scotland, the West Coast Main Line faces the formidable climb of ten miles at 1 in 100 from Beattock station to the summit. In steam days nearly all trains were assisted in the rear and here we have a Caledonian Railway Class 60 4-6-0 No. 14652 banked by a Caledonian 0-4-4T, No. 15163. The train appears to consist of ventilated vans and containers for meat traffic. (L3729)*

LEFT, : *The interior of a slip coach van showing the emergency hand brake screw, lever for releasing the slip-coupling (behind the hand brake) and foot pedal to operate the warning gong. (5/95)*

BELOW : *Anther close up of the slip coach 'works'. The couplings in the normal running position and the pivot which allows the hook to drop and release the coupling is situated midway round the hook. (6/34)*

Slip Coaches

The Great Western was probably the largest user of slip carriages which in B.R. days was unique to the Western Region. The last one, the 5.10 pm Paddington to Wolverhampton, detached at Bicester, ran in 1960. The whole operation was rather fraught as it involved a coach or coaches being detached at speed from the rear of a train and being brought to a stand by the guard of the slip portion. There were in effect for a short time two trains in one section which was against all principles of 'block signalling'. The service offered was of course only one way as coaches could not be attached to a moving train.

LEFT, above : *A slip coach is about to be detached from an up train at Reading. The main train is proceeding under clear signals through the up main platform. The coach, with slip apparatus at both ends, is one of six built in 1938. This is one of the last slip coaches to operate being photographed in 1958. (7/50)*

LEFT, below : *The business end of a slip coach showing the slip coupling, vacuum brake and steam heating pipes with self-sealing valves and foot operated gong to warn men on the track and platform staff of the coach's approach. (5/94)*

ABOVE : *A down Bournemouth and Weymouth train on the four track section (now electrified) between Pirbright Junction and Basingstoke approaching Hook in 1953. The first six coaches, including the restaurant car, are for Bournemouth West. The train split at Bournemouth central, the rear portion going forward to Weymouth. The locomotive is 'King Arthur' Class 4-6-0 No. 30743 'Lyonesse' built by the London and South Western Railway at Eastleigh in 1919. The coaches all appear to be of post-war Bulleid design. The signals are the semi-automatic pneumatic type and the down fast line arm has already gone to danger behind the train. Note the other photographer on the right operating what appears to be a large reflex camera. (132/53)*

RIGHT above : *Two views of down trains at Winchfield. A local train bound for Basingstoke consisting of seven corridor coaches. The locomotive s a Class N15X 4-6-0 No. 32332 'Stroudley' which was a rebuild from a London Brighton and South Coast 4-6-4T. The class became redundant when the Brighton Line was electrified and they could not be utilised elsewhere due to their restricted fuel supply. (122/52)*

RIGHT below: The Devon Belle was a post-war development in competition with G.W.R. trains from Paddington. The service never really caught on due possibly to the supplementary fares charged and it ceased running at the end of the 1954 season. Even by 1952 the patronage was much reduced and the formation was but five Pullman Cars from Ilfracombe plus the Observation Car. The locomotive is unrebuilt 'Merchant Navy' 4-6-2 No. 35021 'New Zealand Line' in dark green livery. (120/52)*

ABOVE : *Swindon works with a valuable collection of brass lying around. This is 'A Shop', the principal building where larger locomotives were repaired. At a general overhaul engines were completely stripped down and all components were refurbished or renewed as necessary. The number plates were thoroughly cleaned and polished before being returned to their respective cab sides. (10/33)*

RIGHT : *Each of the 'big four' railway companies had their own distinctive style of nameplate. The Great Western used separate brass letters and brass beading fixed to a curved steel sheet which was mounted over the middle coupled wheel splasher. The G.W.R. named all its four cylinder express passenger locomotives and the two cylinders mixed traffic 4-6-0s of various classes. These names became a bit monotonous especially when there was a class of 329 engines, all but one named after the stately homes of England.*
'The South Wales Borderers' No. 4037 was one of the 'Castle' class not named after an ancient fortification. It also carried the regimental badge below the nameplate. (17/494)

ABOVE : *The stores at locomotive depots as well as keeping the usual spare parts oil lamps etc was home to the locomotive headboards which were carried by all the named express trains in early B.R .days. Here are four such headboards at Camden (London Midland Region) for trains out of Euston. The 'Express Voyager' board is of especial interest as this was used on special boat trains from Euston to Liverpool Riverside in connection with Canadian Pacific liners. (3/67)*

ABOVE : *A typical Southern Railway curved nameplate 'Robert Blake' a 'Lord Nelson' Class 4-6-0 No. 855. The Southern plates also carried the class name in smaller type face under the name. (6/5)*

ABOVE : *Fortunately Maurice Earley did not ignore the changing scene, , as these four views are now historic. The up 'Mayflower', carrying its headboard, in Sonning Cutting just west of the A4 bridge. The locomotive, No. D602 'Bulldog' was one of five A1A-A1A diesel hydraulic locomotives (Tops Class 41) built by the North British Locomotive Co. in 1958/59. They were not a success and all were withdrawn in December 1967. (32/59)*

BELOW : *The prototype 'Deltic' was tested on the London Midland and the Eastern Regions but was never taken into B.R. stock. It was, however, the precursor of the successful Class 55. It was built in 1955 and on withdrawal in 1961 was placed on display in the Science Museum. Deltic was moved to the National Railway Museum at York in October 1993. It is seen here passing Holme on an up express in 1959. (53/59)*

ABOVE : *The Southern Region produced three 1Co-Co1 diesel electric locomotives which also ran on the London Midland Region. The second of the three, No. 10202, is seen hauling the down 'Bournemouth Belle' at Winchfield in 1952. The locomotive is not carrying a headboard, possibly due to the lack of suitable brackets, although this was normal practice with steam locomotives. (121/52)*

RIGHT : *The era of the Diesel Multiple Unit had started when Maurice Earley was active with his camera. One of the early Derby-built light weight two car units introduced in 1955 is leaving Peascliffe Tunnel bound for Grantham. The dark green livery was later modified by the addition of yellow panels on the front of the cab as it merged with the green of 'England's green and pleasant land' and presented a hazard to men working on the track. (77/55)*

ABOVE : *The short lived L.M.S. 'Coronation Scot' train has already been illustrated and mentioned on page 23. Here the down train, 1.30 pm from Euston, is seen just north of Northchurch Tunnel between Berkhamsted and Tring. Judging from the pristine state of the locomotive, the first of the five blue streamlined 4-6-2s No. 6220 'Coronation', the date must be early in July 1937. (3701)*

ABOVE : *The London and North Eastern Railway's streamlining was probably the most effective although this was rather negated by the wartime removal of valencing over the coupled wheels to make access to the motion easier. No 60017 'Silver Fox', one of the original four Class A4s built in 1935 for the Silver Jubilee express between Kings Cross and Newcastle is seen leaving Welwyn South Tunnel on the down Tees-Tyne Pullman in 1955.(85/55)*

Four views of L.M.S. trains.

ABOVE : *The location is the Somerset and Dorset Joint line (L.M.S. and Southern) but the train is pure L.M.S. although photographed in B.R. days - just. It is the southbound 'Pines Express' from Manchester (London Road) to Bournemouth (West) near Masbury Summit. The train is double-headed for the climb out of Bath over the Mendip Hills. The assistant engine is a famous Midland Railway Class 2P 4-4-0 No. 509 and the train engine a L.M.S. Class 5 4-6-0. The Somerset and Dorset to emphasise that it was 'different' did not use the standard head lamp code to identify the class of train but used just two codes - the passenger one as seen here and chimney and opposite buffers for freight trains. (147/49)*

BELOW : *Climbing Beattock Bank. A 'Jubilee' Class 4-6-0 No. 5696 'Arethusa' on a Manchester Exchange to Glasgow train. The locomotive is carrying the Caledonian style route indicator at the chimney (both arms horizontal indicates Carlisle to Glasgow Central). The date was 26 July 1936. (873)*

ABOVE : *Beattock Bank again near the summit in 1937. A northbound express, probably a Manchester and/or Liverpool to Glasgow, is hauled by 'Patriot' Class 4-6-0 No. 5538. In November 1938 this locomotive was named 'Giggleswick', after the public school. As there are no Caledonian route indicators visible so the engine has worked through from England. (L3716)*

BELOW : *The down 'Royal Scot', 10 am Euston to Glasgow Central, on Dillicar troughs (Westmoreland) hauled by 'Princess Royal' Class 4-6-2 No. 6211 'Queen Maud'. She was the second daughter of King Edward VIII and married King Haakon VII of Norway. Note the spray caused by the water pick-up apparatus. (3714)*

ABOVE : *Paddington 'cathedral' from the balcony window of the headquarters office's corridor looking through the 'transept'. The refreshment kiosk is on platforms 2 and 3 and they then stretch away to platform 12 beyond the last section of arched roof. The station was opened in 1854 replacing a temporary terminus west of Bishops Road. The station covered an area of 700 by 238 feet and has been extended and altered to cope with increasing traffic over the years but the original style was retained. Isambard Kingdom Brunel was the engineer with architectural assistance from Matthew Digley Wyatt. (53/54/51)*

ABOVE : *Brunel's last and perhaps his greatest masterpiece, the Royal Albert Bridge linking Devon and Cornwall. The bridge still stands very much as built and carrying far greater loads than those in 1859 when it was opened. The total length is 2190 feet with 17 approach spurs and two main spans each 455 feet long. To comply with Admiralty requirements, the main girder spans are 100 feet above mean high water. The present view is spoilt by the road bridge opened in 1961 but Brunel's bridge is a far greater engineer's feat than the new suspension bridge, (6/86)*

LEFT : *The interior of Camden No. 1 signal box, the exterior of which can just be seen in the background of the picture on page 18. The box was an L.M.S. 'Air Raid precautions' structure with a second-hand Webb & Thompson all electric frame which came from Crewe. It was a very busy box with four passenger lines between Euston and Camden and various empty carriage lines as well. The calendar on the wall says August 1956. (3/78)*

BELOW : *The western portal of Box tunnel between Chippenham and Bath. This together with Maidenhead bridge were the two major engineering works on Brunel's original Great Western Railway between Paddington and Bristol. Construction commenced in 1838 after preliminary borings and sinking of shafts in 1836 and 1837 and the tunnel was finally opened for traffic on 30 June 1841. It is on a continuous gradient of 1 in 100 falling towards Bristol. Total length is 1 mile 1452 yards. (195/48)*

ABOVE : *Probably the classic Earley photograph. The down Cornish Riviera in April 1938. The conditions were ideal. Crisp atmosphere, sun and wind in the right direction to lift the exhaust. The locomotive is 'King' Class 4-6-0 No. 6027 'King Richard I'. This may have been taken on a Sunday as there is no evidence of the 1938 Centenary stock which formed the weekday train. (H3600)*

ABOVE : *An early post-war shot on 23 September 1945 again of the down 'Riviera' hauled by the first of the 'King' Class No. 6000 'King George V' which is again proudly displaying its bell presented by the Baltimore and Ohio Railroad during No. 6000's visit to America in 1927. The bell was removed during the war, some say it was stolen by an American serviceman. Some of the coaches are still in the wartime all over brown livery. (Q5238)*

ABOVE : *A slightly later post-war picture, 1947, with all the coaches repainted in proper chocolate and cream. Again the down Cornish Riviera hauled by No. 6012 'King Edward VI'. There is someone looking out of the cab and waving. Maurice Earley's negative register is annotated Allen so I presume he is Cecil J Allen the well known train timer. (5331)*
BELOW : *Each year the G.W.R. published a guide to resorts on the railway which also included lists of hotels and boarding establishments. To help popularise their resorts and give people an opportunity to inspect prospective 'digs' special trains were run at cheap fares on Sundays during the late winter and early spring appropriately named Holiday Haunts Express. Here is one such excursion to the West Country on 21 April 1938 hauled by No. 6025 'King Henry III'. These trains must have been popular as this one stretches beyond the road bridge and must have consisted of at last 14 coaches. (A512)*

The main locomotive workshops on the G.W.R. where complete overhaul and construction was undertaken were at Swindon intermediate repairs were tackled. This view is the interior of one such workshop at Old Oak Common, London in 1959. leading railway bogie. The other locomotives visible are Hall Class 4-6-0 no 6939 'Calveley Hall', 61xx 2-6-2T No. 6145, 22

verhampton and Caerphilly. In addition to these facilities a number of the more important sheds also had workshops where
romotive on the extreme left appears to be a King Class 4-6-0 undergoing piston and valve examination and repairs to the
ass 0-6-0 No 2282 and a 56xx Class 0-6-2T. (9/34)

ABOVE : *An up express leaves Reading behind Saint Class 4-6-0 No. 2949 'Stanford Court'. This class was the pioneer 'modern' Great Western express passenger locomotive. The first member of the class was No. 100 (later 2900) 'William Dean' built in 1902. A total of 77 were built between 1902 and 1913. They were all modernised over the years including fitting of superheaters (the last 25 were superheated when new). The photograph was taken in the immediate post-war period. Witness the camouflage paint on the Earley electricity power station on the right. (227/96)*

RIGHT, above : *During the year there are peaks of traffic both passenger and freight. One such, in the late summer was broccoli from Cornwall for which numerous special trains were run as this vegetable which required speedy transit to arrive at the markets in good condition. One such special is seen ascending Hemerdon bank east of Plymouth in 1934. The locomotive is Hall Class 4-6-0 No. 5998 'Trevor Hall' and the train consists of suitably cleaned cattle wagons which were ideal. (50/54)*

RIGHT, below : *In the late 1950s, the Western region were allowed to paint some B.R. mark 1 coaches in the old G.W.R. chocolate and cream livery. These were made up into complete trains and used on the more important named expresses The up 'Torbay Express' from Kingswear to Paddington is seen here leaving Greenway tunnel soon after leaving Kingswear behind a Castle Class 4-6-0 No. 5011 'Tintagel Castle'. (25/59)*

ABOVE : *Greenwood signal box was an important regulation point at the end of the four tracks from Kings Cross where they merged into two for Hadley Wood tunnel. The signals on the up road are still Great Northern somersaults on a lattice post. This was taken on one of Maurice Earley's photographic outings on this day in the company of F. E. Mackay, a well known railway photographer in the 1920s and 30s. Note the heavy equipment which photographers used. This is a camera with a focal plane shutter and rising front which took glass plates. From the size of camera and diameter of the lens the plates may have been whole plate size $8\frac{1}{2}$ x $6\frac{1}{2}$inch or at least 7 x 5 inches. (FIA/30)*

ABOVE : *Up until about 15 years ago the railways also operated shipping services to the continent and Ireland as well as shorter ferry routes. In many cases they also owned the ports and harbours. One such was Folkestone and we see here the harbour station which was approached by 1 in 30 incline from Folkestone Junction. The main line can be seen crossing Foord Viaduct in the left background. The vessel is SS Canterbury which was built in 1929 as a first class only ship for the Golden Arrow service from Dover to Calais. It was later used on the Folkestone-Boulogne route catering for both first and second class passengers. (225/96)*

ABOVE : *The G.W.R. owned a large fleet of road motor vehicles for collection and delivery of parcels and freight to non-rail connected premises and at Theale in Berkshire the company also were involved with the Theale and Great Western Sand and Ballast Company which worked gravel pits about half a mile from the station. A wonderful collection of high side tipping lorries are pictured in Theale station yard in 1930. These conveyed sand and gravel from the pits for loading onto rail. The vehicles include a Foden steam wagon, an unidentified tractor and trailer, at least five Thornycroft four ton lorries on solid tyres, a ten ton six wheel Thornycroft on pneumatic tyres and on the extreme right an Associated Daimler also on solid tyres. (5463)*

ABOVE : *During the 1950s and 60s, railway enthusiast's societies organised many special trains which travelled over unusual routes and often included visits to workshops. One such was arranged by the Railway Correspondence and Travel Society on 25 April 1954. The train started and finished at Victoria and the itinerary included a visit to Swindon works also a trip down the Highworth. The return route was via the wartime connection between the Great Western and Southern Railways where the G.W. locomotive, 47xx 2-8-0 No. 4707, was replaced by ex-London and South Western Class H16 4-6-2T No. 30517 which worked the train to Clapham Junction. It is seen passing Maurice Earley's home station of Earley! (17/54)*

RIGHT, above: *The Southern Railway never carried as much freight as the other three railways as it served mainly residential and agricultural areas. There was, of course, some goods such as shipping traffic via Southampton, domestic coal etc. A Class H15, 4-6-0 No. 482 is heading down the South Western main line near Hook with a Bournemouth line freight train in 1946. (0/5095)*

RIGHT, below : *One of the ugliest British locomotive classes was Oliver Bulleid's Q1, 0-6-0 which was built during the 1939-45 war to a very austere specification. No. 33018 of this class, allocated to Feltham shed, is, if the headcode is to be believed, hauling a Feltham to Wimbledon freight via Chertsey. The location therefore is Virginia Water with the junction signal off for Chertsey. (1/55)*

ABOVE : *The Great Western had a large traffic in coal from South Wales to London via the Severn Tunnel. To work these trains William Dean designed a class of double framed 2-6-0s which were built between 1900 and 1907. No. One is seen on the up relief line near Woodley Bridge signal box on 30 January 1927. The wagons are owned by a mixture of collieries and coal merchants. (853)*

BELOW : *In 1939 the War Department requisitioned 100 Dean 0-6-0s for use in France, most of which were lost after Dunkirk. To replace them G.W.R. received on loan 40 L.N.E.R. Class 25, 0-6-0-s and 43 Midland Railway Class 2F, 0-6-0s. L.M.S. No. 3196 heads a short freight from Reading Central goods near Southcote Junction in 1943. (5020)*